www.thegreatchiweenie.com

ISBN-13 978-0-9814900-3-8
ISBN-10 0-9814900-3-4

All Photographs by:
Cubby Cashen and
Todd Potter.

WARNING: Riding a bicycle can be dangerous. Please wear all
safety equipment and follow all the laws and regulations when
riding a bicycle. Gu is safely harnessed into the backpack in which
he rides, but is still at risk of injury due to any accidents or falls.
Wear a helmet. PLEASE RIDE SAFE. Kayaking can be dangerous
too. RESPECT THE OCEAN.

Teachers, Principals, and Businesses, for bulk purchasing or promotionals,
please contact Cubby at thegreatchiweenie@hotmail.com.

The Great Chiweenie presents

SEA FOR YOURSELF

by GU and Cubby Cashen

The Great Chiweenie Productions
P.O. Box 669
Cambria, CA 93428
thegreatchiweenie@hotmail.com
www.thegreatchiweenie.com

Note from the Author:

Hey! My Name is Gu, a.k.a. "The Great Chiweenie" (Act like the I is silent CH-Weenie). I am part-dachshund and part-chihuahua and I travel with my adopted parents, Megan and Cub. Megan had to be at school on this day, but loves to kayak in the Cove. She along with Hannah Campbell were my scientific fact checkers. This is my third picture book, but this time we had help from Todd (owner of Sea For Yourself Kayaks). He leads tours at the cove and has rentals too. If you're in the area (San Simeon, Cambria, or Big Sur), you can check out his website: kayaksansimeon.com. Hope you enjoy!

Kayaking the cove
is special for those
whose summertime goal
was to be sprayed by a hose.

I avoid water
whenever I can.
But with Cub and Todd
we left the warm sand.

The few on the pier
laughed and pointed my way.
Straight through the waves
I tried avoiding the spray.

I was cold at first,
but slowly that changed.
My seat was all wet,
so I had to rearrange.

There were birds singing,
and a seal took a glance.
I was staring at the shore
just hoping for that chance,

to jump onto dry land
and survive the day.
But Cub grew excited
listening to Todd say,

The water was clear,
with animals all around.
I started to enjoy
the ocean's little towns.

15

We then started back
boats pointed to land.
We went between waves
till we finally touched sand.

19

"We're done! We're done!"
I shouted with glee.
Sebastian's for lunch
is where I wanted to be.

THE END

28

This is a kelp forest. Kelp is a type of algae that can be found in many products we use daily including: toothpaste, cosmetics, ice cream, cereals and milk.

Any part of the kelp can produce food from sunlight through the process called PHOTOSYNTHESIS.

The kelp forest provides homes for many ocean animals. You can find many types of fish, snails, brittlestars, urchins and even sea otters in the kelp.

Giant kelp can grow up to 2 feet a day.

Otters have more hair follicles in one square inch than YOU and your housecat have on their entire bodies.

Sea Otters must eat about a quarter of their body weight each day to help keep them warm.

Otters enjoy eating abalone, sea urchins, sea stars and many other shelled creatures of the sea.

Sea Otters are commonly found wrapped up in the kelp to help keep them (and sometimes their babies) from drifting away while resting.

Other books from
THE GREAT CHIWEENIE
Productions

Picture Books   Chapter Book

www.thegreatchiweenie.com

Keep up to date on all of our new adventures at www.thegreatchiweenie.com. Check back often.

Adopt a pet.
Ride a bike. (or paddle a kayak)
Smile.